SEBASTIAN
BACH
The Boy from Thuringia

SEBASTIAN BACH
The Boy from Thuringia

BY

OPAL WHEELER

AND

SYBIL DEUCHER

Illustrated by MARY GREENWALT

E. P. DUTTON & CO., INC. NEW YORK

TABLE OF CONTENTS

MUSIC

Chapter I
IN THE THURINGIAN VILLAGE
OF EISENACH

THE TOWN CRIER ran down the winding streets of the little German village of Eisenach calling his good news.

"Make way! The band is coming! Make way for the Bach musicians!"

The town-folk gathered quickly under the leafy trees of the beautiful Thuringian village for they were always eager to hear the music of the band.

Almost all who played, — brothers, uncles, cousins, were named Bach.

Down the street came the men, keeping time with their feet to the strong, stirring melodies, their instruments shining brightly in the morning sun.

On they marched, the town-folk following, until they came to the edge of the Thuringian forest,

9

where they stopped to rest by a running stream. The children were tired, too, for they had been running to keep up with the long strides of the men.

It was very beautiful in the cool deep forest with the great Wartburg Castle high above them on the mountainside.

The children begged for one more melody from the band and again the music echoed through the mountains. Then the men led the way back through the winding streets to their homes.

In this same little village of Eisenach, nestling on the edge of the forest, a little boy was born many years later.

When he was only two days old,

to explore the great castle high on the mountainside.
Here, in olden days, the minstrels had sung and
played to entertain the lords and ladies of the castle.

The children climbed the high wall and looked
down.

"Be still! be still!" cried Sebastian "we can hear
their music!" And as they listened they heard plainly
the strong melodies of the older Bachs far below.

In the evening the instruments were brought out

17

and by candlelight the men played the new compositions of one of the Bachs, written since the summer before.

"Bravo! Bravo!" cried the listeners, when they had heard the new music.

Doors and windows of the Bach home were opened wide so the village folk could hear. Indeed, there were so many musicians that some were standing with their instruments in the doorway, for there was not enough room in the little cottage for them all.

Sebastian was sleepy and he rubbed his eyes to keep awake. But it had been too long a day and off to bed he stumbled, the stirring melodies of the players sounding in his ears.

The next day there was music from morning until night. On the third day the festival ended and it was time for the visitors to go back to their homes, so the Bachs were up early and when

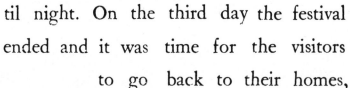

18

all was ready, they came together for a last quodlibet.

"Goodbye, Goodbye," called Sebastian, running excitedly about the horses. He was sorry to see the last carriage drive off, for now it would be a whole year before they would be back again to play and sing together.

When Sebastian was eight years old he was sent to school. It was not long before he was singing in the scholars' choir, for his voice was pure and sweet. Every Sunday the boys sang in church, and on festival days and sometimes for weddings. Very often they marched through the streets singing their songs while the townfolk gathered to hear them. They were very proud of the choir which had been started one hundred years before Sebastian was born.

The great churchman Martin Luther had sung in

the streets when he was a boy, and now Sebastian was singing the same kind of stern chorales that Luther and his followers had sung so many years before.

A very unhappy time came for Sebastian when he was almost ten. Both his mother and father died and he was sent to live with his brother Christoph, who was fourteen years older and lived with his wife and children in Ohrdruff. Christoph played the organ in the church and Sebastian went there every Sunday to sing in the boys' choir and to play on his violin. He was sent to school to the Lyceum where he learned Latin, Greek, singing, and arithmetic.

Christoph taught him to play on the clavier, which

was like a small piano. He was allowed to practice only one hour a day. This was never long enough and he would like to have played on and on as long as he wished.

In Christoph's home there was a large library of music.

"May I use the books? I will be very careful of them," said Sebastian.

"Oh, no,— you are not old enough yet. Some day,— perhaps," answered Christoph.

Sebastian learned his piano compositions by heart very quickly and begged for more difficult music.

"You cannot play the masters yet, Sebastian. Learn the simpler music first and some day you shall have harder compositions to play."

Sebastian was not satisfied. He must have more difficult music. But how could he get it? His brother had already taught him all that he could and yet Sebastian wanted to learn more.

In the high cabinet was a special book of compositions of the masters, but Christoph kept it tightly locked and carried the key in his pocket.

Every day Sebastian walked by the cabinet and stopped to look at the thick black book which he could see through the metal lattice bars.

"Take me down! Only take me down and I will tell you all my secrets," the book seemed to say.

Sebastian looked at it longingly. Again he asked Christoph to let him see it, but this made his brother angry.

One cold night when all the house was dark and still, Sebastian lay in his bed thinking about the book filled with music. He got up quietly and

22

crept to the top of the stairs. Everyone must be asleep, for there was not a sound.

It was cold on the stone floor and he shivered. He started down the dark stairs, feeling carefully for each step. They creaked and he stood still, fearing that someone had heard him.

He reached the last step and moved slowly toward the cabinet. Yes, there it was! He found a chair and climbed up carefully where he could reach the door.

Squeezing his hand between the wire bars he rolled the book up tightly to get it out. With a strong pull it was free and Sebastian was so excited he could scarcely move.

If only he could get back to his room without anyone hearing him!

He climbed the dark steps slowly so they would not make a noise. His room at last! But how could he see

to copy the music? There was no candle, and even though he had one, someone might discover him. The moonlight flooded his little room. Of course, it would be his light!

He quickly found pen and paper and sat in the deep ledge of the window where the moonlight fell

upon the music. Even then it was difficult to see the notes, but he bent down closely and copied from the book as fast as he could. The moon shone for only a short time and it was dark again; so he could work no longer.

He slowly began the journey back to the cabinet, and again forcing his hand between the bars, put the book safely back. Then he climbed the stairs again, crept into bed and was soon fast asleep.

The next day he was tired and the lesson at the clavier did not go very well. His fingers stumbled and he leaned his head on his hands to rest. His eyes smarted. He had to rub them to keep awake.

"Whatever is wrong with you, Sebastian? You have never made such mistakes before," said Christoph.

Sebastian dared not answer and tried to do better so that his brother would not learn his secret.

Every night when the moon shone, he went quietly down the long stairs in the cold to the little cabinet, copied the notes as quickly as he could, put back the big book and crept wearily to bed.

Christoph could not understand the swollen, red eyes of his younger brother who oftentimes went to sleep in the middle of his lesson.

For six long months Sebastian worked and at last the night came when the great task was finished.

When he stole back with the music book for the last time, he said to himself:

25

"It is mine now! I will play every note!"

He could have shouted for joy to think that the great treasure was really his own! He put the music under his pillow and slept soundly.

The next evening when his brother was at the church playing the organ for a special service, Sebastian hurried to the clavier with his book and played the music. But soon hearing footsteps, he ran quickly away just as Christoph opened the door.

The next day the older brother was again at the

church and Sebastian played the music, hurrying away just in time.

But when the third night came, the door opened suddenly and there stood Christoph, angrier than Sebastian had ever seen him.

"What is the meaning of this? So you took the book and copied the music! Very well, then. Give it to me!"

Sebastian could not move. He was afraid that his brother would really take away the one thing that meant more to him now than anything else.

Christoph snatched the copy book from him.

"No! No! You must not take it! You must not take my music!"

But Christoph took no notice of the trembling Sebastian. He strode away with the copy under his arm.

"It will teach you a lesson you will not soon forget. There shall be no disobedience in my household."

That night Sebastian could not sleep and all the next day he could think of nothing but the treasure that had been taken from him.

The old woman who helped in the household was worried because he looked so unhappy. She patted his head kindly and said to him:

"Never mind, my boy, he may give it back to thee some day."

That same morning, when no one was near, Sebastian went slowly to the clavier. How did the melodies go? He tried to play them.

What! He remembered them? On flew his fingers over the keys. As the music rang through the house, the old serving woman came hurrying in to listen. He was playing every note of the music! No need to be sad now, for the melodies he had copied these many long months were safely locked in his mind where no-one could take them from him.

Sebastian knew now that he must find a way to go on with his music.

He hurried to find the Director of the Lyceum to ask his help.

"There is the fine choir school of St. Michael's in Lüneburg, Sebastian, where you could study music. With your fine voice perhaps you could sing in the church. And your good friend, Erdmann,— he is eager to study as well. Why not go there together, my boy?" said the Director.

To Lüneburg! But it was many miles from Ohrdruff. There was no money, so how could he go? There could be no help from Christoph, for he had children of his own and found it difficult to care for them. And even though there was a way to get there, how could he be sure that he would be taken into the choir school?

There was only one thing for Sebastian to do. He must walk two hundred miles over rough roads to St. Michael's in Lüneburg.

Chapter II
AT ST. MICHAEL'S IN LÜNEBURG

EARLY ONE MORNING, even before the sun was up, Sebastian and his friend Erdmann were on the highway, laughing and talking merrily together.

"Come, let us see how far we can go in one day," cried Sebastian, and they began to run down the steep roadway.

They were on their way to Lüneburg where they hoped the good monks of St. Michael's would take them into the choir school. It was a long, long way to travel and the boys had no money and very little food.

But they were as happy as could be for this was a great adventure.

Over the beautiful countryside of Thuringia they traveled. In the early morning light German peasants with their heavy carts were already on their way to near-by market towns. The chimes from the belfry of an old church sounded through the valley, waking the villagers for the new day.

On they went past great fields of heather already in bloom, watered here and there by narrow streams that cut deep channels in the roadway.

It was long after mid-day when they stopped to rest under a great fir tree to eat the small lunches of black bread and sausage that they had brought for the journey. There was little time to rest with so many miles to go so they started off again along the dusty highway.

"Look, Sebastian," cried Erdmann, "There comes an old man with a mule and cart. If only he would ask us to ride with him!"

The mule came jogging up the hill and stopped when it reached the boys. The little man nodded to them.

"Been traveling far? You look a bit weary. If you are going my way, better get in and ride with me."

"Oh, thank you, sir. We're on our way to Lüneburg," answered Sebastian.

"To Lüneburg! Well! Well! That's a long way! Almost two hundred miles! Not going there myself, but I'll take you to the next turn in the road."

How good it was to ride, if only for a little way.

The turn in the road came all too soon. They thanked the little old man and again found themselves trudging along.

It grew cold after sunset, and the boys found shelter in an old hayloft for the night. They buried themselves deep in the hay and were soon fast asleep.

Early morning found them on their way again, a little nearer the choir school of St. Michael's. Their feet were sore and blistered for the stones in the road had cut their shoes.

Days and nights passed and finally one evening, as they came to a sharp bend in the road Erdmann stopped suddenly and shouted:

"There, Sebastian! The lights of a village! Surely it must be Lüneburg!"

They hurried on faster.

Indeed it was Lüneburg. After all these long miles

they had come to the end of their journey. They walked through the narrow streets looking for the church.

"Could you tell us, please, where is the choir school of St. Michael's?" Sebastian asked a little old woman at the market square.

"Yes, lad, away to the left is the church, and near it you will find the school."

There stood the fine old building with its red brick tower covered with cap and lantern of green copper.

They quickly made their way to the choir entrance and knocked at the door.

"Suppose they will not take us after our long journey here!" whispered Erdmann.

There was no time for an answer, for the door opened and there stood an old monk in a long black robe.

"Please, sir, will you take us into your choir school? We have come all the way from Ohrdruff and we would like to sing in the church," said Sebastian.

"From Ohrdruff! You walked all the way from Ohrdruff! Come, come inside, my boys, and we shall

see. First you will need food and rest and in the morning we shall hear you sing."

The kindly old monk led the way to a rough
wooden table where the boys were given coarse rye
bread and bowls of hot soup. Never before had anything tasted so good.

The chimes in the bell tower were ringing and the
monk hurried away to the service in the church,

leaving the boys by a warm fire. They were too weary to stay awake for long and soon were asleep under warm feather covers given them by the good monk.

The next day they came before the singing master.

"So you are one of the Bachs," said the director, looking closely at Sebastian. "Your family is known throughout the countryside for its music. But you must sing well to join the choir of St. Michael's, my lad. Now then, let me hear you."

Sebastian read the music so easily and sang with such beautiful, clear tone that the master was delighted. Erdmann was then given his turn.

"Yes, you will both be a great help to us here, my boys. Indeed you may both stay on with us and live in the choir school."

The boys were too excited to speak. To think of living with these kindly people and to be able to study music to their heart's content! They could hardly believe it was true.

So they began their new life at the choir school. Of

course they studied other lessons as well, but Sebastian was happiest when it was time for music.

He worked hard at the clavier and learned so quickly that he surprised the director more each day. Nothing seemed too difficult for him.

The library was filled with music books and Sebastian was free to use them whenever he wished. He was eager to learn more of the great works. He sat poring over the treasures, never wanting to stop. There were not enough hours in the day for him, so he worked long after the other boys were asleep. Night after night the monks found him reading the music books or playing softly at the clavier.

Sebastian's hands were strong and he played smoothly. Everyone used only the three middle fingers when they played at the clavier but Sebastian discovered it was better to use all five.

When he wasn't needed to sing in the choir, Sebastian was asked to play on his violin for the services in the church. He played in the church orchestra as well and

when anyone was absent, he would play on any instrument that was given him.

"Surely someone must have taught the lad! How else could he play the instruments so easily?" thought the director.

He went to Sebastian.

"How would you like to try the organ in the church today, my boy?"

To play on the organ! Sebastian ran to the great instrument high in the choir loft, and putting his fingers on the keys, began to play. The sounds rang through the church. He quickly tried the wooden bars at his feet and as he touched each one, a different tone came. Then he tried hands and feet together and the great chords rang out.

The director was almost as excited as Sebastian.

"The boy must study the organ! He shall have lessons with Herr Böhm of St. John's church. In time he may become a great organist."

Sebastian liked his organ lessons far better than anything else. He spent long hours in the church at the instrument which was not a very good one, but Sebastian kept on working, hoping that some day he might play on a better one.

He liked to compose as he went along. What fun it was to hear his own melodies. Sometimes the music thundered through the church and then suddenly became very soft and died away.

It was not long before Herr Böhm had taught him all that he was able, so Sebastian went on by himself, finding the most difficult music to play on the instrument.

He spent many long hours writing his compositions. Almost every day there was a new one to show to the director.

Here is a lovely minuet that Sebastian wrote. Can you play it?

MINUET

44

Sebastian studied singing every day with the other boys. He liked the beautiful church music that they learned for the services on Sunday and for special days.

He sang in the church for almost three years and then one day he found that his high soprano voice was gone and he could no longer sing in the choir. So he began to play in the church orchestra and to accompany people when they sang, to pay for his lodging at the school.

45

Sebastian had often been told about the great organ master Reinken, who played at St. Katherine's church in Hamburg, many miles away.

"If only I might hear him, how much I could learn!" thought Sebastian.

Of course there was only one way to do this—he would have to walk all the way to Hamburg where the master was giving concerts.

With his violin under his arm he started off early one morning. Miles before him stretched the rolling countryside. It was a long way to St. Katherine's but the thought of the great organist filled his mind and he strode along, eager to reach the city in time for the concert.

He hummed a jolly marching tune to help pass away the hours.

This march that Sebastian wrote you will surely want to hear.

MARCH

48

It was beginning to get dark and Sebastian looked about for a place to spend the night. In an open field on the left was an old cattle shed, and in a short time Sebastian had forgotten how weary he was, for he was soon fast asleep in an empty stall, the cattle on either side of him quiet for the night.

The next morning he was on his way again, with his violin under his arm. He was very hungry and stopped at the first inn by the wayside. Putting the violin under his chin, he played such a jolly melody that people crowded around the door to listen.

"Bravo! Play us another!" cried the travelers, and again came the gay music.

"Come, my boy," called the innkeeper, "Come and have a bite with us."

How good the warm food tasted! Sebastian would like to have stayed on, basking in the heat of the great open fire, but there was no time for he must be in Hamburg in time for the concert.

When he finally arrived in the city he made his way to the entrance of St. Katherine's. The church was

already filled with people, waiting to hear the great Reinken. Sebastian crept behind a pillar at the back of the church and stood there, tired and dusty, waiting for the concert to begin.

Everyone was silent when the master took his

50

place at the organ. When he played, the music sounded like a great orchestra. Sebastian wanted to shout for joy. He forgot the people, the church, even his weariness as he listened to the music.

When the concert was over he did not leave the church. As the people went out, they looked at the boy and wondered why he was standing there, so still.

Long after everyone had left, Sebastian went out into the cool night. He would never forget the beautiful music of the master Reinken.

The next morning he began the long journey back to Luneburg. He did not think of the long miles before him, for his mind was filled with the music that he had heard played by the great master.

After he had traveled many hours he began to feel hungry.

"I will rest here on this bench," he said to himself, and sat under the window of a little inn at the side of the road. He wondered how he could ever walk the rest of the way with such an empty feeling. He could smell the meats roasting and it made him hungrier than ever.

He took the one small coin from his pocket. It was not enough to pay for even the smallest meal, so he put it carefully back again.

Suddenly a window opened above him and something dropped at his feet.

Two herrings' heads! But what were they doing here? Sebastian picked them up and looked at them closely. What was that shining in the mouth of each one? A gold ducat! But who could have dropped them here?

He quickly took the coins and looked about to see who had been so kind to him. There was no one in sight.

"Now I can buy myself a good dinner!" he cried, and hurried into the inn.

Seating himself at a table, Sebastian ate heartily. He felt much better and wished that he might thank whoever had dropped the ducats to him.

After he paid the innkeeper he wrapped the rest of the money in a package and put it safely away.

"I will keep it for my next journey to Hamburg," he promised himself, and started on his way to Luneburg.

Though he was very tired, he went a little faster

so that he would reach the village before sundown.

The boys and the monks at the choir school welcomed him back. After a good warm supper they sat and listened to his exciting adventures.

It would be hard to wait until he could journey again to Hamburg to hear more beautiful music played on the organ by the master Reinken.

A few weeks later Erdmann came to Sebastian with a letter that had just come for him.

Sebastian opened it quickly.

"News! Good News, Erdmann! I am to play at the Duke's palace at Weimar!"

"At Weimar!—What luck for you!" cried Erdmann.

"Yes, I am to leave in the morning. The Duke says that I will live at the court and play every day in the orchestra!"

"We will miss you here at St. Michael's. It will seem strange without you after our three years together."

"But you will come often to Weimar to see me, Erdmann. It is not far away."

The boys hurried to pack a small bundle of clothing so that Sebastian would be ready to start the next morning at daybreak for the Duke's palace at Weimar.

Chapter III
SEBASTIAN'S MANY JOURNEYS

EVERYONE AT ST. MICHAEL'S was up early the next morning when Sebastian was ready to start for Weimar.

After a good breakfast of hot porridge and brown bread, the monks and choir boys gathered about the doorway to see him off.

"Come back soon to visit us, Sebastian!" "Be sure to follow the right road to Weimar!" they called after him.

Sebastian turned to wave to his friends in the doorway. He was sorry to leave the choir school which had been his home for three happy years. With a last goodbye, he came to a sharp bend in the road and was soon out of sight.

This was the beginning of many long journeys for Sebastian for he was to travel far and wide over the countryside of Germany.

As he walked along, he listened to the sounds about him in the woods and meadows. Melodies filled his mind and as he sat by the roadside to rest, he wrote bits of them on paper.

You will want to play this gavotte that Sebastian composed. The gavotte, you know, is a French peasant dance.

GAVOTTE

61

When Sebastian reached Weimar he quickly made his way to the royal court. The orchestra leader greeted him kindly.

"So you are young Bach. Well, then, you will play with the second violins. We are to have a rehearsal early tomorrow morning. Be sure that you are on time."

He was the first one ready the next day, long before it the hour! The men of the orchestra took their places. Sebastian watched the director carefully and played the second violin part without a mistake.

"Be on time tonight at eight, ready for the concert. See that your costumes are in good condition," said the director and dismissed the men for the rest of the day.

Sebastian could hardly wait for the evening to come when he would see the Duke and other royal members of the court.

When the hour arrived he took his place, his wig neatly tied and shoes carefully polished.

The royal guests in their rich costumes came into the great concert room. Last of all the Duke, in gay velvet suit with gold braiding, took his favorite chair and the concert began.

When the first number was over, Sebastian eagerly looked about him and was delighted with the lights and splendor of the court.

Again the music sounded through the great hall, the Duke applauding his favorite selections and calling:

"Again, my good men, play that music again!"

When the concert was over and the stands and instruments were put away, Sebastian was free to walk about the vast grounds of the beautiful palace.

The moon shone brightly through the great trees overhead and cast shadows down the long pathways. This beautiful place was to be Sebastian's home for many days.

Often when visitors were presented to the royal family, a solemn processional called the polonaise was played by the orchestra. Sebastian wrote many of these dances and this polonaise of his should be played in a stately manner.

POLONAISE

For several months Sebastian enjoyed the life at the court. One day the Duke sent word that the men would have a short vacation.

Several of Sebastian's relatives lived in Arnstadt, a short distance away and he decided to pay them a visit. He remembered this beautiful little village for it was there that the Bachs had sometimes gathered for their yearly feasts of music when he was a boy.

He made ready at once and was soon on his way. Arriving in the village, he found his uncle's home.

"Sebastian! Come in, my boy, come in! It is so good to see you again! You have come just in time to try the new organ in the church."

"Yes, uncle, I have heard about the new instrument and I would indeed like to play on it. The organ is the greatest instrument of all."

68

Word was sent about the village that Sebastian was to play in the church, and when the day came, the people waited eagerly to hear him.

Sebastian seated himself at the fine new instrument and a great chorale sounded through the church.

This young man had rare power! The people could hardly believe that such beautiful music could be composed while they listened.

When the concert was over, the leaders of the church hurried to him.

"Herr Bach, we enjoyed your music so much that we would like you to be the organist of our church and the choir director as well."

Sebastian could not believe the words! To be the organist of a church and to lead a choir of singers!

69

"Yes, I will be glad to come if the Duke of Weimar will permit me to leave his orchestra. It would be a real pleasure to play on such a fine instrument!"

Sebastian did not know that the leaders of the church were very strict people, but he soon learned that this was true.

When the Duke permitted him to leave Weimar to begin his duties at Arnstadt, a special service was held. Sebastian was asked to stand and repeat the words of the stern leader:

"I promise to be a faithful servant of God and a good organist, and I will carry out all of my duties and obey the wishes of the leaders of this church."

But he was happy to live in such a beautiful village and to play for all the services in the church. He could study the works of the great masters, too. But most of all, when there was time, he could compose for the organ.

This fine chorale of his is played in churches everywhere.

CHORALE

Moderato

71

Many times during the church service, Sebastian played on and on, composing as he went along. He forgot when it was time for the people to sing so they did not know when to begin or when to stop.

"You must make your music shorter," said the leaders.

This did not please Sebastian. There were more rehearsals now and this meant that there was not as much time to compose as he wished. But he stayed in Arnstadt for four years, playing the organ, studying, and composing.

One day he decided to ask the leaders for a short vacation.

"I should like to go to Lübeck. The great organist, Buxtehude, is playing some special music there."

"Very well," answered the leaders, "But we will expect you to be back with us in exactly four weeks."

It was good to be free again ! Sebastian walked along in the bright sunshine. There were more than two hundred miles to travel to hear the great organist, but he knew he would be well repaid.

72

The miles seemed never to end, but after many, many days of traveling, he arrived in Lübeck and found St. Mary's church where the great Buxtehude was to give his concert.

When the service began, Sebastian leaned forward, anxious to hear every note of the music. If only he could play like the master some day and perhaps study with him! But there was not enough money, so he must learn what he could by watching and listening.

Every time that Buxtehude played, Sebastian was there to hear him. How much he was learning! It had been so long since he had heard such great music. It swept through him and filled him with the greatest joy.

Three months passed all too quickly, and he had promised to return to Arnstadt in four weeks! He said goodbye to the old master and started the long journey back to his home.

It was winter now and Sebastian trudged through the great drifts of snow that filled all the roadways. It was a hard, cold journey, and he wondered if Arnstadt would ever come in sight.

When he finally arrived, the leaders of the church were very much displeased with him for staying away for three long months. But they knew that no one could play their organ as well as Sebastian, so he went on again with his duties in the church. He worked harder than ever at his composing and playing, for he had learned much from the master Buxtehude, and it was a great help to him now.

This is a part of a jolly gavotte that Sebastian wrote.
You may want to find the music and play all of it.

GAVOTTE

A short distance away from Arnstadt was the little town of Mühlhausen. The people there had heard of Sebastian's playing, and some of them had gone to Arnstadt to hear him. They needed a new director for their music, so they asked Sebastian to be their choir leader and organist.

Sebastian knew that he would have more time to compose if he went to Mühlhausen, so he decided to go there to live with his new wife, Maria Barbara.

It was agreed that the people would give him a cart to bring their belongings to the new little home. Besides his salary, he was to receive corn, wood, and fish for

the year, brought to his door without extra charge.

All was arranged and soon Sebastian and Maria Barbara were comfortably settled in a little house in Mühlhausen.

The people were pleased to have such a fine director as Sebastian for the music in their church.

Several happy months passed in the new home when one day a messenger arrived from the court of Weimar. He came to the house of Sebastian.

"Herr Bach, the Duke has heard of your fine playing and wishes you to come to the court of Weimar to play for the royal company as soon as you can arrive there."

Sebastian hurried to find Maria Barbara.

"Just think, my good Maria! I am to play at the court of Weimar for the Duke and his royal company! It seems only yesterday that I played there in the court orchestra. Of course the Duke will not remember me!"

"But he may, Sebastian. When do you go?"

"As soon as ever I can make ready. But I shall not be gone for long."

Soon he was on his way in the carriage, jogging along over the rough roads.

The evening that he arrived at Weimar, all the royal company had gathered to hear the young composer, Sebastian Bach.

He came forward and bowed to the royal guests, seated himself at the harpsichord, which was like a small piano, and began to play. Everyone listened eagerly to his music. The Duke leaned forward and looked closely at Sebastian. Surely this was very rare. Never had anyone played so beautifully in his palace.

When the music was ended he sent for Sebastian.

"My dear Bach, indeed you must be the same young man who played in my orchestra only a few years ago. And your own compositions,— they have delighted me. I should like to have you come here to live and be my court organist."

To think of being the chief organist at the royal court of Weimar !

The Duke was waiting for an answer.

"I thank you for this honor, sir. I shall tell the people of Mühlhausen of your kind offer and they will surely allow me to leave. Then I shall make arrangements to come to Weimar as soon as possible."

Maria Barbara was delighted when Bach told her of the new position at the royal court, and in a few weeks they had moved to Weimar and were comfortably settled.

They were very happy in this beautiful place where they lived for nine long years.

Sebastian and the men of the orchestra had many duties. Besides giving concerts, they waited on the Duke. They were sometimes footmen, cooks, or huntsmen. On special occasions they were dressed in bright Hungarian costumes and served the Duke and his guests at royal banquets.

But Bach's most important duty was to write music to be played and sung in the court chapel.

The town-folk were delighted whenever word was sent to them that they might hear a concert by Sebastian Bach. They crowded into the small chapel to hear the beautiful organ music and great cantatas that he had written.

Year after year Bach became better known throughout the countryside. Only one other German composer was said to equal him. His name was Handel, and he had gone to live in England.

80

This little musette was written by Bach to sound like bagpipes playing.

MUSETTE

The private organist to the King of France was visiting in Germany at this time. His name was Marchand. The French people thought him the greatest organist and harpsichord player in the world. Indeed he was the organist of several of the largest churches in Paris.

He went to Dresden and presented himself at the splendid court of King Ferdinand Augustus, where he hoped to astonish everyone with his playing. The King and members of the royal court were delighted to have the noted French organist as their guest and spent long evenings listening to his music.

"You must hear our great German musician, Sebastian Bach," said King Augustus to Marchand.

Suddenly an idea came to the King. Why had he not thought of it before? There should be a contest between these two musicians to see which was the better player!

A messenger was sent with all speed to Weimar inviting Bach to play with the famous Marchand. Bach liked exciting adventures and hurried to Dresden to the court of the King.

Chapter IV
THE CONTEST WITH MARCHAND

THERE WAS GREAT EXCITEMENT in the city of Dresden over the contest between Bach and the French musician, Marchand.

Everyone wondered which of the two men would be judged the greater master.

It was late in the afternoon when Bach arrived at the court of King Ferdinand. He was warmly greeted by an old friend, Volumier.

"Come, there is just time to reach the concert hall where Marchand is playing for the last time before the contest on the morrow."

"Indeed I would like to hear him," said Bach, and they hurried to the great room where the audience was seated.

In a few moments Marchand came in, richly dressed in court costume of brown velvet and costly lace. On his fingers were handsome jeweled rings.

He bowed low to the King and the royal company and began to play on the beautiful harpsichord. When he finished, a round of applause filled the room.

The King was surprised when a courtier whispered to him that Herr Bach was in the hall. He looked about eagerly and saw the master sitting at the far end of the room.

"And now, Master Bach," called the King, "Will you be good enough to show us a little of your skill before the contest tomorrow?"

"With pleasure, your Majesty," answered Bach, bowing low.

He made his way to the front of the room and took his place at the instrument. Turning to the King he said:

"If your Highness will give me a short melody, I will use it for a composition which I will play for you now."

The King was greatly interested and gave Bach a little melody and the master made it into a fugue, weaving the melody in and out.

"Bravo! Bravo!" cried the audience when it was finished.

All the time that Bach was playing, Marchand listened closely to every note. He knew that here was a great master indeed.

The day of the concert arrived and the excitement at the court was greater than ever. Count Flemming had offered his beautiful music room for the contest and all was in readiness. A costly new harpsichord had been placed at one end of the long gallery for the great event.

Opposite were three chairs where the King, Queen, and Crown Prince were to sit.

The judges chosen for the occasion were among the finest musicians in all Dresden. They were seated on a raised platform in gay court costume waiting eagerly for the contest to begin.

Bach entered the room dressed in a plain black suit and large white wig. He carried a small black hat under his arm. People looked at him and smiled. Indeed this was no court costume in which to appear before such noble company!

A long trumpet call announced the King and Queen, the Crown Prince, and lords and ladies in waiting.

A little page dressed in royal blue called in clear tones:

"The first musician to the King of France, Jean Louis Marchand, will be the first to play in this contest!"

Everyone looked around for the first view of the richly dressed French musician.

There was a long silence. Where was Marchand? Count Flemming was upset at the delay and ordered the estate searched for the missing Frenchman. Word came that he was nowhere to be found, so a messenger was sent with all haste to his hotel. He returned quickly.

"Your Majesty, I have been told that Marchand left Dresden early this morning by fast coach."

89

The Count was much disturbed and tried to explain to the King.

"Well, Herr Bach," said his Majesty, "Then you must begin. Now you will have to surpass yourself!"

Bach seated himself at the beautiful new instrument and played with such skill the royal company was astounded.

"Well, well, my good Bach, you made up entirely for Marchand's absence. You are indeed a master of the harpsichord and a great composer. You have delighted us all."

The next morning he sent Bach one hundred gold pieces with a kind letter telling him again of the pleasure he had received at hearing him play.

Just as the master was about to leave the court of the King, Prince Leopold of Cothen came to him.

"Master Bach, I enjoyed your playing at Count Flemming's so much that I would like to have you come to live at my court to play the organ and violin.

Of course you would have ample time to compose. Would you care to come?" asked the Prince.

"Yes, indeed. I have often heard the Duke at Weimar speak of you and your love for music. I am sure I would enjoy being at your court."

There would be much to do in the Bach household to get ready to leave for Anhalt-Cothen. Bach was eager to tell Maria Barbara the good news.

You will enjoy this lovely Minuet in G that Bach wrote.

MINUET

Chapter V
THE HOME OF THE BACHS

THE GAY LAUGHTER of the Bach family rang through the house as the children ran about from room to room packing their few belongings to take to their new home in Anhalt-Cöthen.

"Come, Friedemann and Emanuel, help me strap the last box to the carriage and we can be off," called Bach to the two older boys.

The smaller children came running to see if they could help.

"I fear it is too heavy for you, little ones, but perhaps you could help your mother with the luncheon," said their father.

Everyone in the Bach household had been busy all morning for there had been much to do to get ready to leave for Anhalt-Cöthen.

"The carriage is here! At last we can start," called Maria Barbara.

Bach lifted the younger children carefully into the high carriage and when Maria Barbara was comfortably seated, he climbed to his place beside the driver.

It was a bright sunny day for the ride. Bach laughed and sang with the children as the horses galloped along the road to Anhalt-Cothen.

For several hours they journeyed through the quiet countryside where meadows stretched for miles on either side of the roadway.

The children were delighted when they came to a great forest. Suddenly the tall pine trees shut out the noonday sun and it grew darker and colder as the carriage went deep into the wood.

They were glad when they came out again into the

warm sunshine and the horses drew up at the side of the road. Everyone climbed down from the carriage for it was time for lunch and they were hungry after riding in the crisp air for so many hours.

"Come, children," said Maria Barbara. "Here is bread and cheese and a bit of sausage for each of you."

"We have still many miles to go, so we must not stay here too long," said Bach.

When the last bit of sausage had been eaten, they quickly climbed into the carriage and were off again.

It was quite dark when they came to the end of their journey and found the house where they were to live. Candles were lighted and the children were hurried off to bed, weary after their long ride.

Bach and Maria Barbara put the little house in order for the night. This was to be their home for six long years.

In a few days Bach was at work composing and directing the music at the court of Prince Leopold. The Prince was younger than Bach and grew very fond of the master. Many times he asked his help about important matters of the royal court.

When Prince Leopold went on long journeys, he always took his organist with him. This pleased Bach very much for he liked to travel more than anything else. He enjoyed going from one beautiful place to another in the satin cushioned carriage. Often they would be gone for weeks at a time.

One day Bach decided to go on a short visit to Hamburg to see the aged organ master, Reinken.

"Perhaps you would like to make the journey with me," he said to his two older boys.

Friedemann and Emanuel were overjoyed for they had often heard their father speak of the great musician.

They eagerly set out in the carriage. When they arrived in Hamburg, word went about that Sebastian Bach, the organist of the Prince of Anhalt-Cöthen was in the city.

At once invitations came to him asking him to play in almost every church in the city. He gave many concerts and was especially pleased when he was invited to play at the church of St. Katherine's, where so many years before he had listened to the music of the master Reinken.

Bach sat with the boys near the organ loft of the old church. Now he was to play on the same great organ for the evening concert!

"Often I journeyed to this very church over long rough roads to hear the organ master when I was a boy, not many years older than you, Friedemann," said Bach.

100

"But how did you come so many miles?" asked Emanuel.

"Always on foot," answered their father. "You see, there was no other way for me to make the journey."

By this time the church was filled with people waiting to hear the noted visitor, Sebastian Bach.

Friedemann and Emanuel sat in the audience while their father made his way to the organ.

The people listened spellbound throughout the concert. Their own beloved Reinken, now an old man, had come to hear the music. He came forward slowly when it was over.

"My dear Bach, I thought there were no longer masters of the organ, but I am mistaken. You alone have the power to make it speak."

Bach and his sons spent the night as the guests of the aged Reinken, where before a bright fire, the younger musician told the old master of his early struggles to study music.

Everyone hoped that Bach would remain in Hamburg

to be the organist in one of their churches, but he soon journeyed back to Anhalt-Cöthen with his two sons, and was again at work at the court of the Prince.

This is part of a jolly jig that Bach wrote. You will see how the left hand repeats the theme that is first played by the right hand.

GIGUE

103

After six years were spent in the service of Prince Leopold, word came from the city of Leipzig asking Bach to be the choir master at St. Thomas' School.

He gathered his children about him and told them of the new position in the great city.

"And you, Friedemann and Emanuel, you are growing older now and should have a fine education which is not possible here in Anhalt-Cöthen. Would it not be well for us all to go to live in Leipzig?"

"Oh, yes!" cried the children, "Let us go at once!"

And so before many weeks had passed, Bach and his children were living in the great city of Leipzig.

The duties of the choir master, or cantor of St. Thomas' School were many. Besides teaching the boys to sing and play on instruments, Bach taught them all the music that was sung in the church and for special festivals.

104

There were lessons in Latin to be given as well and this was not so pleasant, for the boys were very mischievous and tried the patience of their cantor until he became very weary. But there was nothing to do but to go on with his work at the school for Bach had many children and it was necessary to keep the position to make a living for them all.

His new wife, Magdalena was a great help to him in his trials. After Maria Barbara had fallen ill and died Bach had been sad until Magdalena came to bring joy to his home. She had a beautiful voice and Bach loved to listen to her sing.

Indeed there was always music in the Bach home for all the children studied music with their father. He was very patient with them and carefully explained the difficult places in the music until they became easy. They all learned to play on instruments. Everyone, even

the littlest, read the most difficult music at sight.

"Come, Friedemann, you shall have this clavier book. I will write new melodies in it for you to practice."

Friedemann enjoyed the pieces that his father wrote for him. He learned them quickly and Bach was kept busy, writing new ones each day. Friedemann sometimes lost one of the pieces from the notebook and his father would say:

"Well, then, I must write another."

He wrote this little bouree for Friedemann's clavier
book. A bourée is a cheerful old French dance.

BOURÉE

Allegro moderato

Magdalena too, had lessons with the master. Bach kept a little notebook where he wrote clavier pieces for her to play.

This gay musette was written especially for her notebook.

MUSETTE

109

After the evening meal, when Bach had spread large slices of brown bread with honey for his hungry children, he helped Magdalena with the dishes and then hurried to work in the little garden while it was still light. When darkness fell he romped with the children before they all gathered for evening prayers.

"Now, then, it is time for bed," he called and helped Magdalena with the littlest ones.

When all was quiet, Bach and Magdalena sat at the wide table with tall candles to give them light. Until long past midnight they worked together copying music to be used for the services at the church, for it was far too costly to have it printed.

Often there was a fretful child to care for and Bach left his work to rock the little one and softly hummed his lovely chorale.

BESIDE THY CRADLE HERE I STAND

Be - side Thy cra - dle here I stand, O

Thou that ev - er — liv - - - est, And bring Thee with a

"Now, Magdalena, we must stop, for you are tired. We will finish tomorrow," said Bach.

Many times after he had gone to bed a new melody would come into his mind and he would hurry to the harpsichord to play it before writing it down.

This is the theme of a beautiful melody that he wrote for stringed instruments. It is often played as a solo on the violin and is called the Air on the G String.

Bach often traveled about the countryside giving concerts, for his earnings at St. Thomas' were too small to take care of his large family,—there had been twenty children! He liked especially to visit beautiful Thuringia where he had lived so many years before.

One evening Magdalena was busy at her spinning wheel. Bach and the children were gathered about the harpsichord, singing and playing when a loud knock sounded at the door.

A messenger had arrived from the Elector of Saxony.

114

"Herr Bach, His Royal Highness, the Elector, sends greetings with this message."

Bach took the large scroll and carefully broke the gold seal. He smiled and handed it to Magdalena.

"Children! A great honor has come to your father. He has been given the title of Court Composer to the Elector of Saxony."

The children shouted with joy and danced around their father. They were so happy that the honor had finally come to him for which he had waited so long a time.

Friedemann and Emanuel were especially delighted and went with their father when he was given the title.

The two boys had been studying hard at their music for many years and were now ready to earn their living as fine musicians.

Bach was very proud and happy on the day when Emanuel was given the position of Court Musician to King Frederick the Great. Emanuel was soon at the palace of the King at Potsdam enjoying his new work.

115

He spoke often of his father and the King wished to meet the great composer, whose music he had often heard.

A special invitation was sent to Bach inviting him to the palace. He was delighted that he would soon see his son and with Friedemann began the journey to Potsdam.

King Frederick the Great was very fond of music and liked to play the flute with his orchestra. An evening concert was about to begin at the palace when the King was handed a list of visitors who had just arrived at the royal court.

He looked at the paper and putting down his flute, exclaimed:

"Gentlemen, old Bach has arrived!"

He sent word for the master to come at once to the hall. Bach came into the room in his dusty traveling clothes, explaining that he was sorry not to appear in court costume.

116

"But my dear Bach, that is nothing. Come, you must see my fine new instruments and then you shall play for us," said the King.

He led the master through the long halls where costly harpsichords were placed. Bach played on all seven of the beautiful instruments and then asked the King to play a theme so that he might make it into a composition.

The King played a short melody on his flute and Bach wove it into such a beautiful composition that when he had finished the King exclaimed:

"There is only one Bach!"

The master enjoyed his visit with Emanuel at the royal court and was soon on his way home again with Friedemann.

It was evening when they neared the little house in Leipzig. They could hear the lovely voice of Magdalena singing a beautiful song that Bach had written.

117

MY HEART EVER FAITHFUL

Andante con moto

My heart, ev-er faith-ful, Sing prais-es, be joy-ful! Sing

prais-es, be joy-ful, Thy Fath—er is near! My

heart, ev-er faith - ful, Sing prais - es, be joy - ful! Sing

prais - es, be joy - ful, Thy Fa - - ther is here!

119

"Welcome home, Sebastian and Friedemann. We have indeed missed you," said Magdalena, greeting them at the door.

How good it was to be at home again!

"Whatever could we do without you, Magdalena! You take such good care of us all," said Bach.

As much as he liked to travel, Bach was always happiest at home with his family and friends about him. Though he had many cares, he forgot them all when he was composing.

When the day's work was over, he liked to walk out into the night alone, through the woods or by the winding river where he could watch the moon and stars. Beautiful melodies would come to him and he would hurry home to write them down on paper.

All of his works for the organ, harpsichord and stringed instruments was the beginning of music as we know it today. It was a pathway for other great composers to follow.

The Bach home was the meeting place for all who loved music. Rich and poor alike gathered there with their instruments to play and sing together or to study with the master who was loved and respected by everyone.

Around a crackling fire on cold winter evenings the good friends came to play the music of the master. Even the littlest ones shared in the evening concerts.

"Bring more candles, Magdalena. Another log on the fire, Friedemann, and we shall begin," cried Bach.

Through the long winter evening in the bright candlelight they played the great works of the master, the strength and beauty of the music giving them all the greatest joy.

"It is growing late. We must have a song and dance from your jolly 'Peasant Cantata' before we go," said a young neighbor.

The children were quickly ready for a merry dance as the older ones played and sang:

Now Let Us to the Bagpipes Sound.

NOW LET US TO THE BAGPIPE'S SOUND

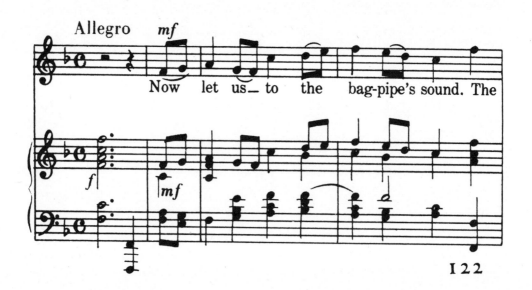

122

merry, merry, merry, merry, merry, merry, sound, Dance out a measure

let us to the bagpipe's sound, The merry, merry, merry, merry,

merry, merry, sound, Dance out a meas - ure gay.

"Good-night, my good friends. We must have another concert soon. You are always welcome at the home of the Bachs."

The master stood in his doorway holding a candle high to light the snowy pathway.

So his music was a ray of light for those masters who were to follow and is to us, now, who listen to the music of Johann Sebastian Bach.